ENERGY SOURCES

Facts · Issues · The Future

NUCLEAR POWER

NEIL MORRIS

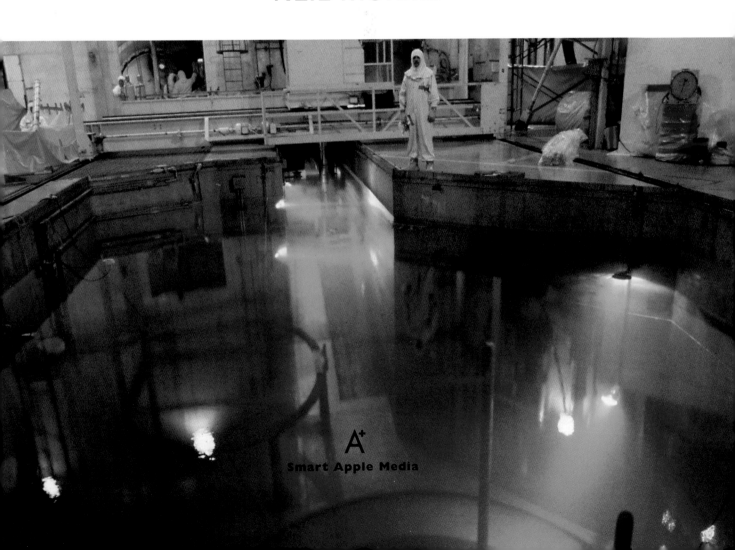

A⁺

Smart Apple Media

Published by Smart Apple Media
2140 Howard Drive West
North Mankato, MN 56003
Designed by Guy Callaby
Edited by Mary-Jane Wilkins
Illustrations by Graham Rosewarne
Picture research by Su Alexander

Photographs by
Page 1 Tim Wright/Corbis; 4 Charles E Rotkin/Corbis; 6 Bettmann/Corbis;
7t Andy Hibbert;Ecoscene/Corbis, b Bettmann/Corbis; 8 Bettmann/Corbis;
9 Corbis; 10 Craig Aurness/Corbis; 11t Yann Arthus-Bertrand/Corbis,
b Corbis; 12 Adam Woolfitt/Corbis; 13 Christopher J Morris/Corbis; 14 Roger
Ressmeyer/Corbis; 16 Vladimir Repik/Reuters/Corbis; 17 Bettmann/Corbis;
18l Bettmann/Corbis, r B.S.P.I./Corbis; 19 Corbis; 20 Bettmann/Corbis;
21t Bettmann/Corbis, b Roger Ressmeyer/Corbis; 22 Roger Ressmeyer/
Corbis; 21t Reuters/Corbis, b Roger Ressmeyer/Corbis; 24 Roger Ressmeyer/
Corbis; 25 Alain Nogues/Corbis Sygma; 26 Tim Wright/Corbis; 27t Dan
Lamont/Corbis, b Jim McDonald/Corbis; 28 Pete Saloutos/Corbis;
29 US Department of Energy/Science Photo Library; Front cover: Jim
Zuckerman/Corbis

Printed in China

Library of Congress Cataloging-in-Publication Data

Morris, Neil, 1946-
Nuclear power / by Neil Morris.
p. cm. — (Energy sources)
Includes index.
ISBN-13: 978-1-58340-907-7
1. Nuclear engineering—Juvenile literature. 2. Nuclear
energy—Juvenile literature. I. Title. II. Series: Morris,
Neil, 1946- Energy sources.

TK9148.M675 2006
333.792'4—dc22 2006003277

First Edition

9 8 7 6 5 4 3 2 1

Contents

Energy from matter

Nuclear power comes from the energy stored inside atoms. These are the tiny particles from which everything around us is made.

Atoms are the building blocks of all substances. Every atom has a central part, called a nucleus, which is where the word "nuclear" comes from. We can use nuclear energy to provide the power to run machines, as well as to light and heat our homes, offices, and factories.

The term "energy" comes from the Greek word *energos*, meaning active or working. Energy sources help other things become active and do work, such as lifting or moving objects. For example, nuclear power can be used to make electricity. So when you turn on an electric light in your home, the energy to make it work might have come from a nuclear power station.

The control room of Calder Hall, in northern England, which became the world's first full-scale nuclear power plant in 1956. This photograph was taken a year later.

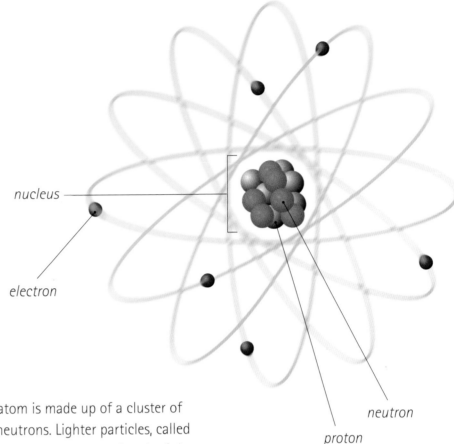

This diagram of the inside of an atom shows the three different kinds of particles.

nucleus

electron

neutron

proton

Inside an atom

The central nucleus of every atom is made up of a cluster of particles called protons and neutrons. Lighter particles, called electrons, circle around the nucleus. The atoms of each of the world's elements—such as carbon, gold, hydrogen, oxygen, or uranium—contain a different number of protons. The metal uranium, which is the most important element for nuclear energy, has 92 protons, while hydrogen has just one. But each element can have different numbers of neutrons. The most common form of uranium has 146 neutrons and is called uranium-238 (or U-238 for short) because it has a total of 238 protons and neutrons.

Releasing energy

Some elements have unstable atoms, which means that their nuclei can break apart. When they do so, they give off particles and energy before forming a more stable nucleus. The elements that can go through this process naturally are known as radioactive elements. Uranium is radioactive, and the form known as U-235 (with 92 protons and 143 neutrons) is least stable and releases the most energy when its nucleus breaks apart. We produce nuclear power by purposely breaking apart the nuclei of unstable atoms.

NONRENEWABLE RESOURCE

Nuclear power is not a renewable resource, unlike wind, water, solar, geothermal, or biomass power. This is because nuclear fuel is used up to produce power (and the spent fuel is very dangerous). Once we have mined and used all of Earth's uranium, there won't be any more.

Early discoveries

French scientist Henri Becquerel discovered radioactivity in 1896. Becquerel found that invisible rays from a lump of uranium ore affected a photographic plate.

His work was carried on by Polish-born French scientist Marie Curie and her husband Pierre. The Curies studied a metallic rock called pitchblende in their search for the source of radiation. Their studies helped them discover two new metallic elements, which they named radium (from the word "ray") and polonium (after Poland, Marie's homeland).

These exciting discoveries earned Becquerel and the Curies the Nobel Prize for physics in 1903. But scientists still did not fully understand this mysterious radioactivity, and they had little idea of its dangers. Marie Curie herself died of a blood disease that was probably caused by exposure to radiation.

Marie Curie working in her laboratory in Paris in 1905.

The father of nuclear science

At the beginning of the 20th century, scientists still thought that atoms were the smallest particles and that they could not be divided. This changed in 1911, when New Zealander Ernest Rutherford discovered that atoms have a nucleus. He also discovered that the nucleus was surrounded by particles called electrons traveling at incredible speeds. Rutherford's work won him a Nobel Prize, and he is often called the father of nuclear science.

Mass and energy

In 1905, famous German-born scientist Albert Einstein figured out that the mass (or amount of matter) in atoms can change into energy. Later, this led scientists to realize that when a nucleus breaks apart, some of its mass seems to be lost. But it is not really lost—it is just changed into energy. And Einstein figured out that the amount of energy released is enormous. Scientists later discovered that one pound (.45 kg) of radioactive uranium can release more energy than three million pounds (1.4 million kg) of burned coal.

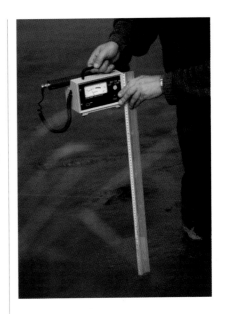

Using a Geiger counter to measure levels of radiation. Hans Geiger, the German scientist who invented the instrument in 1912, was Ernest Rutherford's assistant.

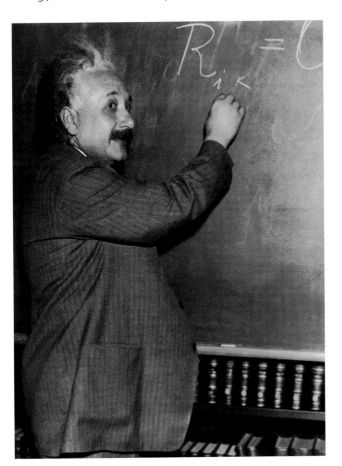

Albert Einstein (1879–1955) developed many ideas and theories. This photograph was taken in 1931. Nine years later, he became an American citizen.

Beginning of the nuclear age

During the 1930s, scientists learned a great deal more about the structure of atoms and their nuclei. They began trying to use particles called neutrons to bombard atoms in an attempt to split the nuclei of the atoms.

In 1939, a group of German and Austrian physicists announced that they had managed to split an atom of uranium. They named this process "nuclear fission" (meaning the splitting of a nucleus). Other scientists started to wonder if the neutrons that split off from a nucleus could be used to split another nucleus and set up a series of nuclear fissions. This is called a chain reaction, and it was first achieved in a controlled experiment in 1942. The experiment marked the beginning of the nuclear age.

Italian-born physicist Enrico Fermi (1901–54) led the team that produced the first successful chain reaction—beneath the stands of a University of Chicago sports field! This photograph shows Fermi eight years later, working with a device called an atom smasher.

The world's first atom bomb was exploded at Trinity Site, in New Mexico. This was the first time anyone had seen the mushroom-shaped cloud produced by nuclear weapons.

The Manhattan Project

When the first nuclear chain reaction was created, the world was at war. The United States had entered World War II less than a year earlier. American scientists were already working on using chain reactions to produce the first atom bomb. In 1942, they came together for this purpose in a top-secret program called the Manhattan Project. They were afraid that German scientists might be doing exactly the same thing, so they worked as quickly as possible. Three years later, the Americans achieved their goal and tested the first nuclear explosion in the New Mexico desert.

Calder Hall

At the start of the nuclear age, a lot of scientific work was aimed at producing weapons. But during the early 1950s, great progress was made on using nuclear energy to produce electricity. In 1953, work began on building the world's first full-scale nuclear power plant, in northwest England. The Calder Hall plant started generating electricity three years later. Eventually, four nuclear reactors were built on the site, which operated until 2003. Today, about a fifth of the United Kingdom's electricity is produced by nuclear power.

Mining uranium

Uranium is a very heavy, silvery white metal found in Earth's crust. It has to be extracted from ores obtained from different kinds of rocks.

Uranium was first found in 1789 and was named after the planet Uranus, which had been discovered eight years earlier. The ore was first found in pitchblende rock, which is still the most important source of uraninite, or uranium ore.

Sandstone, shale, and granite rocks also sometimes contain uranium. Most of the ore comes from underground mines, where miners dig vertical shafts down from the surface. Horizontal tunnels lead off from the shafts to the ore deposits, where miners or remote-control drills remove it in chunks. Some uranium also comes from opencast or open-pit mines, where metal is recovered from thick beds of ore that lie close to the surface.

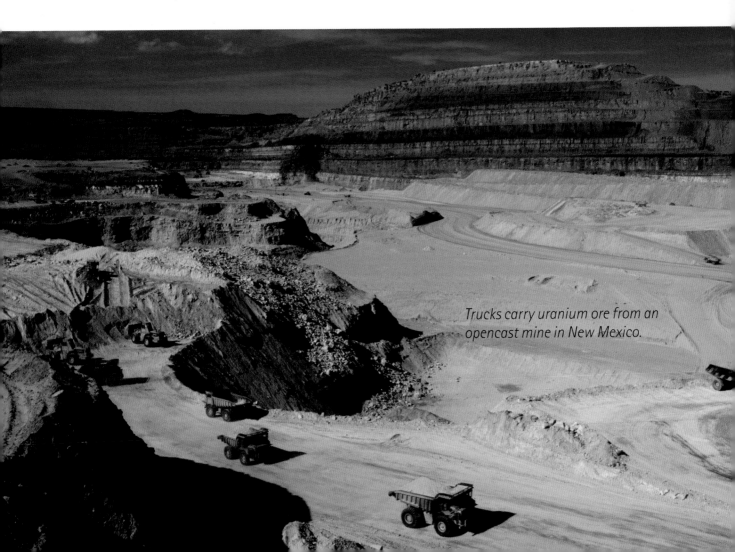

Trucks carry uranium ore from an opencast mine in New Mexico.

From North America to West Africa

Canadian mines produce more than a quarter of the world's uranium. The world's second-biggest producer is Australia, followed by Kazakhstan. Next comes Niger in West Africa, where uranium ore is the country's most important natural resource. Niger exports its uranium, which mainly comes from sandstone rocks and makes up two-thirds of the country's income from abroad. Although all of these countries are rich in uranium, only Canada has nuclear power plants.

This aerial photograph shows some of the sandstone and uranium deposits in an open-pit mining region of Niger. The country also has underground mines.

HAZARDOUS MATERIAL

U-235 makes up less than one percent of uranium, but this is increased to up to four percent at fuel-enrichment plants. Throughout the whole process of mining and using uranium—called the nuclear fuel cycle—special precautions have to be taken so that people are not exposed to radiation or the dangerous chemicals used in the process.

Uranium-235

Uranium ore is crushed, ground, and treated with chemicals. This produces a substance called yellowcake, which mainly contains the most common isotope (or form) of uranium, U-238. Small amounts of the more useful U-235 are separated so that this isotope is increased. This is a complicated process, and one step involves spinning the material around very fast in a machine called a centrifuge.

A sample of U-235 powder.

Generating electricity

Nuclear power plants generate about one sixth of the world's electricity. Just like coal-fired plants, they use energy to create heat and produce steam to drive a generator.

Rather than burning fuel, a nuclear reactor (see pages 14–15) uses a chain reaction of splitting nuclei to create the heat energy needed to boil water. Special precautions are taken to make sure that all radioactivity stays within the reactor, which is inside a three-feet-thick (1 m) concrete and steel structure called a containment building, which is often dome-shaped.

Nuclear power plants need a great deal of water, both to make steam and to cool the system, which is why they are usually built near a sea, lake, or river. The electricity generated is carried along power cables to towns and cities. The cables are often held high above the ground by tall pylons.

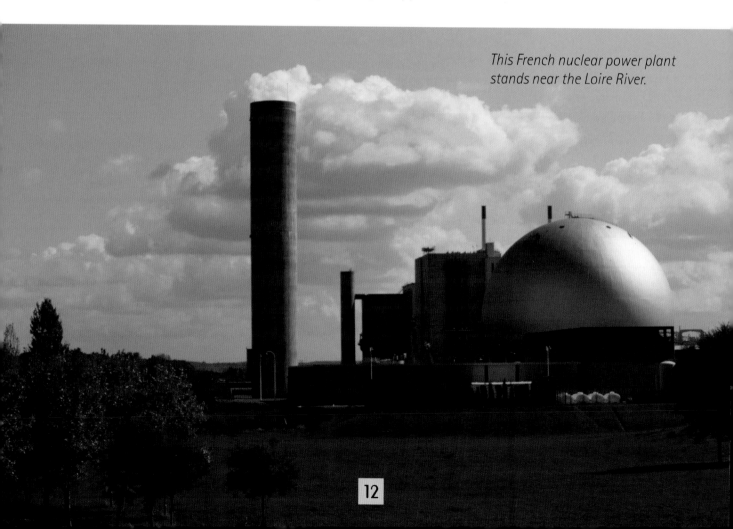

This French nuclear power plant stands near the Loire River.

Turbines and generators

The idea of generating electricity began in 1831, when British scientist Michael Faraday discovered that he could create electricity by moving a magnet through a coil of copper wire. This led to the invention of the generator, which works by changing mechanical energy into electrical energy.

In a nuclear power plant, the power of high-pressure steam provides mechanical energy by hitting the blades of a turbine and turning them. The blades are connected to a shaft that is attached to a generator. Inside the generator, the shaft makes magnets spin inside wire coils to produce electricity.

In the control room

All of the operations in a nuclear power plant are monitored in a central control room. Many operations are fully automated, but experienced controllers constantly check that everything is happening exactly as it should.

If there is an emergency, computers shut down the reactors and other equipment, and it is impossible to override them. Today, many nuclear-power companies have simulators so that operators can practice controlling a power plant. The simulators are like those used by airline pilots, and nuclear engineers can use them to practice emergency protocol.

These turbines are driven by the steam from a reactor in a California nuclear power plant.

Nuclear reactors

The central structure of a nuclear power plant is the reactor, and inside it is the reactor core.

The core contains nuclear fuel, which is made up of metal rods containing pellets of uranium. These are surrounded by a liquid or gas that carries heat away to boil water and make steam. Some reactors use water as a coolant; others use carbon dioxide gas.

In the reactor core, the nuclear fuel releases neutrons that break other nuclei and start a chain reaction. Control rods are inserted into the core to slow down the reaction. The rods are usually made of boron, which absorbs neutrons. The rods can be moved in and out of the core, slowing down or speeding up the nuclear reaction. A separate set of shutdown rods can be inserted into the core to stop the reactions quickly if there is an emergency.

The four reactors of the Paluel power plant on the coast of northern France are contained in domes. They are connected to turbine and generator buildings. This power plant opened in 1985.

Pressurized water

There are several different kinds of nuclear reactors, although they work in a similar way. More than half of those operating in the world are pressurized water reactors (or PWRs for short).

Inside the PWR containment building, the reactor heats water under great pressure, which allows it to get hotter than normal before it boils. Heat from this water boils different water in a steam generator. The high-pressure water is pumped back to the reactor, where it is heated again. Steam drives the plant's turbine before cooling, changing back into water, and returning to the steam generator.

Fast-breeder

There are a few experimental fast-breeder reactors in the world. They get their name because they "breed," or make, more nuclear fuel as they react. They are called fast because they do not slow down neutrons. Other kinds of reactors do this to make the particles more effective at breaking nuclei.

EFFECTIVE BUT RISKY

Fast-breeder reactors have been developed in France, Japan, and Russia, and they may be used in India and China. But there have been problems with fast-breeders, and many environmentalists consider them more dangerous than other reactors. In 1995, there was a leak of sodium coolant at the Monju fast-breeder in Japan. No one was hurt, but the reactor has been shut down ever since.

This diagram of a pressurized water reactor shows that the two water systems are separate.

steam generator

turbine

electric generator

condenser

reactor

Dangers and accidents

In the early hours of April 26, 1986, a reactor began
to fail at a nuclear power plant in the Soviet Union.

The reactor should have shut down
automatically, but operators had
switched off the safety device to run
a test. Within seconds, there was a
massive power surge, followed by
an explosion that blew the top off
of the reactor and the roof off of
the containment building.

The plant was at Chernobyl, north
of Kiev, in what is now the Ukraine,
and it was the world's worst nuclear
accident. The explosion and fire sent
large amounts of radioactive material
into the atmosphere. No one knows
exactly how many people died in the
accident, but many thousands were
killed or made seriously ill by the
effects of the nuclear fallout. Many
were in the Ukraine and neighboring
Belarus and Russia, but the effects
of radiation were felt in many other
European countries, too.

The Chernobyl accident was so
frightening that it made many experts
question the use of nuclear power.
The following year, for example, the
people of Italy voted to close down
their nuclear power plants.

*The damaged Chernobyl reactor in
1986. It was later sealed in concrete.*

Three Mile Island

In 1979, there was a serious accident at the Three Mile Island plant near Harrisburg, Pennsylvania. A cooling pump failed, and the pressurized water reactor shut down automatically. However, a valve stayed open, and the reactor core overheated as fuel rods began to melt.

The reactor's containment building did not break or burst, but there was concern for some time that radiation might have escaped from the plant. Safety experts ensured that rules and procedures at nuclear power plants were tightened up. A report later concluded that some radiation had escaped.

The Three Mile Island plant is on the Susquehanna River. Reactor number 2 was shut down and has never reopened, but reactor number 1 is still in operation.

Destructive weapons

The first nuclear weapons of the 1940s were atomic bombs. These bombs worked by creating nuclear fission and allowing a huge chain reaction to take place.

On the ground, a shock wave was followed by a fireball and then radioactive fallout. American warplanes dropped two atomic bombs on Japan in 1945, with devastating results.

The next weapons were H-bombs (hydrogen bombs), in which the nuclei of hydrogen atoms were forced together. These fusion bombs were even more destructive than fission bombs, and many of today's nuclear weapons work this way.

Besides bombs, some modern armies have nuclear missiles, mines, and torpedoes. An international agreement called a non-proliferation treaty aims to stop nuclear weapons from becoming more widespread and

A mushroom cloud towers up to 20,000 feet (6,000 m) over Nagasaki on August 9, 1945. Japan surrendered five days later, ending World War II.

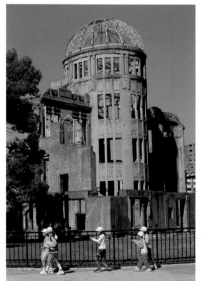

Japanese schoolchildren walk past the Memorial Dome in Hiroshima. Those who died in the city are remembered every year on August 6, Hiroshima Day.

works towards nuclear disarmament. Five countries that have nuclear weapons have signed the treaty—Britain, China, France, Russia and the U.S.—along with 182 others. A few countries, such as India, North Korea, and Pakistan, have declared that they have nuclear weapons but have not signed the treaty.

Hiroshima

At 8:15 on the morning of August 6, 1945, an American B-29 bomber dropped an atomic bomb on the Japanese city of Hiroshima. When the bomb reached a height of 1,830 feet (560 m) above the city, an explosive inside it drove one piece of uranium-235 into a larger piece. The massive nuclear blast killed up to 100,000 people, injured many more, and destroyed about 5 square miles (13 sq km) of the city. The heat from the blast was so intense that it burned everything in its way, including people. Three days later, a plutonium bomb was dropped on Nagasaki, with similarly devastating effects.

Modern missiles

Nuclear missiles are made up of a rocket with one or more explosive sections called warheads. They are guided by on-board computers, and large missiles can travel thousands of miles. Some have been specially developed to be launched from submarines, which are difficult to detect or follow as they move beneath the world's oceans.

An American nuclear missile being tested off the coast of Florida.

On the move

During the 1950s, people believed that nuclear power could be used to drive all sorts of vessels and vehicles.

Nuclear power was first (and most successfully) used in submarines. The power system was very similar to that of a nuclear power plant. In a nuclear submarine, a reactor produces steam to drive a turbine that turns a propeller shaft and pushes the vessel through the water.

Unlike other systems, a nuclear engine needs no air and uses very little fuel. One pound (.45 kg) of uranium produces more energy than 2.5 million gallons (9.45 million l) of diesel oil. A nuclear submarine can stay underwater for a very long time. In 1960, the twin-reactor *U.S.S. Triton* remained submerged for 84 days as it traveled all the way around the world. Nuclear engines are also used for icebreaker ships.

This is how the future looked in 1958. The Ford Nucleon concept car was designed to be powered by its own self-contained nuclear reactor. The dangers of nuclear power meant that it never took to the road.

U.S.S. Nautilus

The first nuclear-powered submarine, the *Nautilus*, was launched in 1954. On its early voyages, *Nautilus* broke all records for time and distance traveled underwater. Then, in 1958, it made a historic voyage to the North Pole, where it arrived beneath the ice with a crew of 116 men on board. On the voyage, *Nautilus* traveled under the frozen polar ice cap of the Arctic Sea for nearly 1,860 miles (3,000 km). *Nautilus* went on breaking records for 25 years before being turned into a museum on the Thames River in Connecticut.

The U.S.S. Nautilus was 320 feet (97 m) long and 26 feet (8 m) wide.

Space travel

Many deep-space probes have been powered by small nuclear devices called radioisotope generators. Apollo lunar astronauts also used such generators to power scientific instruments on the moon.

FASTER THROUGH SPACE

American space engineers are working on nuclear-powered unmanned spacecraft, which they hope will visit some of the icy moons of the planet Jupiter. In the future, nuclear power could be used by humans to travel to Mars. Burning rocket fuel, the journey would take six months. Nuclear fuel could cut the space journey to two months.

This illustration shows a possible future Mars spacecraft.

Nuclear fusion

Nuclear fusion (meaning "uniting" or "joining together") is the opposite of fission. Fusion occurs when the nuclei of two light atoms combine to form a heavier one.

For fusion to happen, the nuclei must be moving at a very high speed, and this requires an extremely high temperature. This is the process that powers the stars. Fusion is called a thermonuclear reaction, and this is what takes place inside an H-bomb (see page 18).

The fusion of one pound (.45 kg) of light nuclei releases more energy than burning 40 million pounds (18 million kg) of coal. A lot of research has been done in hopes of producing a fusion reactor that could generate electricity. Nuclear engineers have built several test reactors, but so far they have not proved practical.

A test fusion reactor called a tokamak. *The Russian name means "doughnut-shaped chamber." This reactor can produce a temperature of 920 million °F (510 million °C).*

Energy of the stars

All of the stars we see in the night sky are huge, hot balls of gas that give out light and heat. We see the light as twinkling pinpoints. New stars are being born all the time, and their energy is produced by nuclear fusion. The same is true of our very own star, the sun, which gives us all the energy we need to survive on Earth. At the center of the sun, in its core, the high temperature (about 27 million °F, or 15 million °C) and density (about 100 times the density of water) cause the nuclei of hydrogen atoms to combine to form the nucleus of a helium atom. At the same time, an enormous amount of energy is given off and takes just over eight minutes to travel through space and reach Earth.

New stars are being formed by nuclear fusion in this spiral galaxy. The photograph was taken by the Hubble Space Telescope.

Laser technology

Scientists at a laboratory in California used a powerful laser-driven reactor to produce fusion. The huge laser, called Nova, operated from 1985 to 1999. It produced pulses of laser light, which traveled in beams down 10 long, tubular arms and were then concentrated on a single one-millimeter spot. An incredible amount of power in the form of light and heat was concentrated on nuclear fuel for just a billionth of a second, which was long enough to cause nuclei to fuse.

The operators in the middle show the size of the Nova laser device at the Livermore National Laboratory. Altogether, the laser was as long as a football field.

Around the world

The production and use of nuclear-powered electricity vary greatly around the world. More than 400 nuclear reactors generate electricity in about 30 countries.

More power plants are planned and being built in some places, while others have reached the end of their useful lives and are being shut down. At the beginning of the 21st century, Europe produced well over 40 percent of the world's nuclear power. North America generated less than a third, and Asia about a quarter of the world total. There is only one nuclear power plant on the continent of Africa (in South Africa), just three in South America, and none in Australia. The U.S. is the leading national producer of nuclear power, followed by France and Japan.

Power cables carry electricity from the two reactors of the Diablo Canyon power plant on the Pacific coast of California. Nuclear power generates a fifth of America's electricity.

INTERNATIONAL CONCERNS

Iran plans to open a nuclear reactor, and in 2005, Russia agreed to supply the Iranians with help and nuclear fuel. The U.S. and other countries were concerned about this because they were afraid that Iran might use the fuel to build nuclear weapons.

Workers in anti-radiation suits inspect equipment at a plant in southern France.

Europe

Belgium, France, Lithuania, Slovakia, and Sweden—all European countries—use nuclear power to generate more than half of their electricity. In France, the figure is more than three-quarters, which means that the country depends heavily on its 59 reactors. The French government decided to build many more nuclear plants after the world oil crisis in the 1970s. At the same time, French scientists have done a great deal of work to improve nuclear technology. France also exports some of its electricity to other countries, including Italy, which has no nuclear plants.

Increasing production

Many new reactors are planned in several Asian countries. Japan is by far the biggest producer, followed by South Korea, where a further 8 reactors are planned in addition to the 20 already producing electricity.

Benefits and problems

One of the advantages of nuclear power is that it produces a huge amount of energy from a small amount of fuel.

Nuclear fuel lasts much longer than coal, natural gas, or oil. Another advantage over fossil fuels is that nuclear processes do not release carbon dioxide and so do not pollute the air or add to the problems of global warming. But there are big disadvantages, too. The two most important are the problems of waste and possible accidents.

Many people think that these negatives outweigh the positives and that nuclear power simply has too many dangers. Another worry is the link with nuclear weapons, and the possibility that terrorists or dictators might get hold of nuclear material and use it for the wrong purpose.

You can see the control rods (see page 14) in the cooling pool of this nuclear reactor. The technology works well, but is it too dangerous?

THE PROBLEM OF WASTE

After it has been used in a power plant, nuclear fuel is much more radioactive than it was before. The material may remain radioactive for hundreds or thousands of years. So it is important to dispose of it safely, but where? At the moment, most spent fuel is stored at or near nuclear plants. Some may be reprocessed and reused, but this is very dangerous. Most experts believe that the best long-term solution is to bury the waste deep underground, in places where there is no danger of earthquakes or floods. Today, some nuclear waste is still sent to other countries by ship or train, causing protest from people who say this is extremely risky.

These drums are filled with nuclear waste before being buried in underground trenches. The symbol stands for radioactive.

These demonstrators in Germany are protesting plans for a new nuclear power plant.

China syndrome

Many people are concerned about the dangers of nuclear plants. The greatest fear is that a reactor might reach a point known as "meltdown" and that nuclear fuel might burn through its protective building. In the 1970s, this led to a new term, "China syndrome," which suggested that a reactor core might burn its way right through the earth from the U.S. to China. A film by the same title was made in 1979. Nuclear experts consider this to be impossible, but no one can ignore the potential dangers.

Future trends

During the second half of the 20th century, many experts believed that more and more people would use nuclear power all over the world.

Today, the situation appears very different. Some nations are planning to build more reactors, but others are shutting them down and banning further development. At the same time, demand for electricity continues to increase and environmentalists point out the pollution hazards caused by power plants burning fossil fuels.

A RISK WORTH TAKING?

Are the benefits of nuclear power worth the risks? Many feel that more effort should be put into renewable energy sources, such as wind and water, and their use will surely increase in the future. People must also learn to use energy more wisely and sparingly, as scientists go on looking for new ways to exploit the world's energy sources.

A patient is treated in a linear accelerator. This produces high-energy radiation to treat cancer.

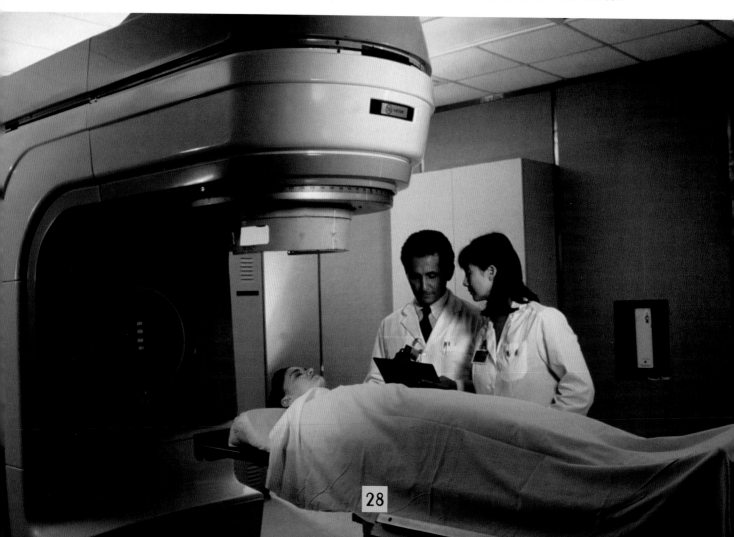

Nuclear medicine

This branch of medicine may develop new techniques in the near future. Today, specialists can use radioactive materials to detect and treat certain diseases. Patients may be given tiny amounts of a radioactive substance, which shows up inside the body on special scanners. In radiotherapy, cancer cells are attacked by X-rays or particles of radium or other radioactive substances. New machines are being invented that are more precise, and perhaps these will be even more effective later this century.

Weapons of mass destruction

Many countries have signed agreements not to build more nuclear weapons (see page 18), not to make any at all, or not to test new weapons.

Many environmentalists and peace protesters would like to see all nuclear weapons destroyed. Everyone knows that a nuclear war would have disastrous consequences for our planet. The possible link with weapons also stops many people from supporting the production of nuclear fuel. This debate will continue to be vitally important in the future.

This underground nuclear test site in Nevada was photographed in the 1960s. International agreements may ban such tests throughout the world in the future.

29

Glossary

anomaly An event that is different from normal.

atom The basic particle of all matter.

atomic bomb (or atom bomb) A device that releases explosive, destructive power created by the fission of substances such as uranium-235 and plutonium-239.

chain reaction A series of continuing reactions (such as nuclear fission) in which each one causes the next.

containment building (or structure) A strong, often dome-shaped structure containing a nuclear reactor.

control rod A rod that absorbs neutrons and can be put into a nuclear reactor to slow down fission.

core The central part of a nuclear reactor.

electron A particle in an atom that circles the nucleus. It has a negative electric charge.

element A substance that cannot be separated into a simpler form.

environmentalist A person who is concerned about and acts to protect the natural environment.

fallout Radioactive dust created by a nuclear explosion.

fast-breeder A nuclear reactor in which neutrons are not slowed down and nuclear fuel is produced as it reacts.

fission Splitting an atomic nucleus.

fuel enrichment Increasing the amount of a more radioactive isotope in nuclear fuel such as uranium.

fusion Joining together atomic nuclei.

Geiger counter An instrument that measures radiation.

generator A machine that turns mechanical energy into electrical energy.

global warming Heating up of Earth's surface, caused in large part by pollution from burning fossil fuels.

hydrogen bomb (or H-bomb) A device that releases explosive, destructive power from the fusion of forms of hydrogen.

incident A dangerous event.

isotope The form of an element with a particular number of neutrons (such as uranium-235, which has 143 neutrons).

laboratory A room with special equipment for scientific research.

laser A device that generates an intense beam of light.

mass The amount of matter in something.

meltdown Overheating of nuclear fuel so that a reactor core melts.

mine An explosive device that goes off when it is touched.

missile A weapon propelled by a rocket and directed by remote control or on-board computer.

neutron A particle in the nucleus of an atom; it has no electric charge.

non-proliferation Preventing the increase or spread (of nuclear weapons).

nucleus The central part of an atom.

off-site Beyond or outside a nuclear plant.

opencast or **open-pit mine** A mine in which ore is extracted at or near Earth's surface.

ore Rock or mineral containing a useful metal or valuable mineral.

pollute To damage with harmful substances.

power plant A plant where electricity is generated.

proton A particle in the nucleus of an atom; it has a positive electric charge.

pylon A tall metal tower that supports power cables.

radiation Energy given out in the form of waves from radioactive substances.

radioactive Describes a substance such as uranium that has unstable atoms that give off energy in the form of waves or streams of particles.

radioactivity High-energy particles given off by radioactive substances.

radiotherapy Treating disease using radiation.

reactor A device that uses nuclear reactions to release energy.

reprocess To process something so that it can be reused.

simulator A device that imitates the controls of a nuclear power plant, used for practice and training.

thermonuclear Relating to nuclear reactions that occur at very high temperatures.

torpedo An explosive device that travels underwater to hit its target.

turbine A machine with rotating blades.

uraninite Uranium ore.

Index